I0148043

Walking in the Light of Heaven

A Journey Through Heavenly Places

You might also enjoy a previous book by Rex Vesey:

Walking on the Shores of Heaven:
A Cancer Survivor's View of the Other Side

With Interpretive Illustrations by Charles Wolfsandle

Published 2011
R & R Publications, Flagstaff AZ
ISBN 978-0-9823727-9-1

Walking in the Light of Heaven

A Journey Through Heavenly Places

Rex Vesey

With Interpretive Illustrations
by Charles Wolfsandle

R & R Publications

Flagstaff

© 2015 by Rex Vesey
All rights reserved. Published 2015
in the United States of America

ISBN: 978-0-9823727-9-1

Cover design and interpretive illustrations by Charles Wolfsandle

R & R Publications
Flagstaff, Arizona
LouellaHolter.com

Dedicated to Everyone Who Desires
Guidance and Love from
the "Celestial Light"

Contents

Foreword

Does Heaven truly exist? If so, how do we get there and what will our experiences be when we arrive? What transformations must we undergo to enable us to enter this mysterious place? What is the purpose of Heaven? Is there a Divine Intelligence at the helm? If so, how do we experience this Divine Intelligence? So many questions! Have you ever asked yourself any of these questions? Well, I sure have, and many more!

You hold in our hands an extraordinary book by an equally extraordinary author. This is a book of profound visions that will both answer your existing questions and provoke new ones. This is not a book merely to be read but rather to be *experienced* by the reader through thoughtful meditation. Before I say more, let me tell you a story steeped in the energy of this book.

In October of 2012, amid the excitement of class reunion planning, the subject of a favorite teacher naturally arose, and without hesitation the name Rex Vesey popped out of my mouth. This was not the first time I'd thought about Mr. Vesey over the past forty-five years; there were many occasions over the years when an old class photo or sixth-grade treasure had sent my thoughts his way. And a quick Internet search revealed a book on Amazon written by Rex Vesey, called *Walking on the Shores of Heaven*. Could it possibly be *that* easy to find him after all these years? Yes, it was! The book's back cover revealed a photograph of my beloved teacher with his kind eyes and warm smile, indicating that he still lived in Arizona. My desire to someday reconnect with the teacher who left such a lasting impression on my sixth-grade psyche was soon to be a reality. I quickly ordered two copies of his book.

I've often wondered what the determining factor is in the connection between two human beings. Why does the essence of some become etched in our memory while others pass through without leaving a mark? For me Rex Vesey is one of those memorable connections. He was an amazing, young teacher in the sixties with many thought-provoking ideas and practices, some of which were not always embraced by the school administration. His students loved him! We were treated as "little brothers and sisters" with the utmost respect for our personhood. When I read *Walking on the Shores of Heaven*, I quickly understood the connection. It was spiritual! It was energetic! Even back then he was practicing honoring the "Holy Presence of God" within himself and others.

The book you hold in your hands, *Walking in the Light of Heaven*, reveals my teacher's personal journey through heavenly places. Through a series of visions you will be transported to Heaven, experiencing the cleansing and attunements necessary for our spirits to enter the "Empyreal Hall," where we interact with other "soul-beings" and, in my humble opinion, form lasting bonds with these beings. Your spirit will recognize them in the future because of their "beautiful radiance which characterizes them in a unique way, being adorned with garments of light matter."

In this book, you will have multiple opportunities to experience the light and love of God, right now. In the Choral Forest you will be soothed like the gentle rocking lullaby of a loving mother. The Sea of Fields provides an energetic cleansing from the inside out while grounding and harmonizing the spirit. Through Energy Falls you can experience a re-energizing awakening of the spirit in preparation for Archways of Energy Mists and so on, as each place prepares you for the next. The ability to fully verbalize these concepts is to have experienced them.

Rex Vesey has a unique ability to translate spiritual experiences of energy and light into the scientific world of energy as electrical currents and back to the spiritual in an effortless manor. He is equally comfortable discussing the most cutting-edge scientific research on "wave genetics" by Grazyna Fosar and Franz Bludorf, or Sidney Coleman's wormhole theory, or Austrian physicist Wolfgang Pauli's "Exclusion Principal." I find there is a brilliant flow of understanding in his writing, truly enhanced by experiencing these visions and attunements.

We are left knowing that we have choices in our spiritual development and are urged to consider verbally transmitting "good will" as a spiritual practice and a healing balm. I truly believe that Rex Vesey embodies this practice. I am honored to now call him not just teacher, but friend.

Rená Thornhill, LMT
In-Touch Center for the Healing Arts
Casa Grande, Arizona

Acknowledgments

I gratefully acknowledge, with heartfelt thanks, the kindness, love, and support showered upon me by the following very special persons, all of whom made this book possible.

* Lynn, my wife, whose continuous positive encouragement for all of my writing aspirations has again made this writing project possible. Her excellent suggestions have brought everything together.

* Charles Wolfsandle, who masterfully created the artistic illustrations accompanying my vision descriptions. They are truly inspiring in the way he has grasped some semblance of my perceptions which lie beyond this realm.

* S. A. Mouti, for photographic excellence in producing the author photo for the back cover.

* Rena Thornhill, who has greatly honored me with her kind and masterful writing, expressed in a foreword. Her healing work continues to bless all those who visit her Healing Arts Center.

* Louella Holter, my publisher, who has believed in the value of my writing endeavors and has made this book possible through her kind patience, sharp intellect and organizing skill.

* Malcolm Smith, whose healing energy of mind, body, and spirit has made better the lives of countless people. I am forever grateful to be one of them.

* Manisha Master, my very adept written text organizer and highly proficient word processor.

* Monica Saaty, for back cover jacket organization and design.

* Dr. Marie Hughes and Dr. Robert Calmes, two great Professors of Education who were dedicated to the highest standard of teaching excellence at the University of Arizona. Their special guidance awakened in me the value of exploring the mystical and creative aspects of knowledge as guides toward excellence in teaching.

The Light is all, and in the Light there is only one thing – Eternal Life

– Merlin[1]

Introduction

Have you ever wondered what lies beyond this reality? Undoubtedly, everyone who is alive has wondered what lies beyond the changeover, what we call the afterlife. I greatly desired to answer this question as a result of a very intense, transforming personal experience that occurred during my visit to the MD Anderson Cancer Hospital emergency room in Houston, Texas.

I was recovering from major surgery for prostate cancer when severe pain caused me to rush to the emergency room to check for possible complications. The emergency room was particularly crowded during my visit. I was lying on a rolling hospital bed in an aisle walkway, from which I could observe many patients coming and going from small alcove rooms.

From one doorway emerged a very thin, frail, weak young woman pushing an I.V. stand with at least six bags of medicine. I was so struck by her appearance, observing how cancer had ravished her body, that I felt a sudden rush of compassion surging through me—I was getting well, and she might not. Then, a young man in his late twenties was wheeled right in front of me, also with a number of medicine vials hanging on a pole attached to his bed. Within a short time, a nurse came over and I overheard her saying in a very kind manner, "Your blood platelets are extremely low, and we will have to admit you for several transfusions." A sense of great sadness came over me, realizing that he had life-and-death challenges to cope with every day.

1

That's when I silently asked the question: "What lies beyond the veil of this reality?" I wished greatly to know. Then I felt a strong sense of peace come over me, and a distinct feeling that I might find the answer to that question.

I want to emphasize that throughout my stay at the MD Anderson Cancer Center in Houston, Texas, all staff members without exception displayed a deep sense of caring, devotion, and selfless dedication to me and all the patients I met. I will always remember those beautiful people.

Following my time of treatment there, over a six-month period, I was greatly humbled and honored to receive glimpses of twelve places beyond our reality, which are presented in my first book, *Walking on the Shores of Heaven*. Seven more visions are described in this book, *Walking in the Light of Heaven*. These came to me in the year following publication of my first book. The visions presented in my first book transmitted a very comforting, reflective cognitive impact for soul transcendence. However, this second group of seven visions more specifically describes places with even greater potential for soul growth and spiritual transformation.

The seven visionary places described in this book specifically target opportunities for enhanced refinement and ascension to new levels of perfected soul growth. Each reader may receive a very personalized, "mind's-eye" visualization as they read through the seven vision descriptions. I sincerely hope that this journey will be very comforting and enriching.

Each illustration is the best possible interpretation of what I tried to express in my written narrative. To describe something in a dimension different from our own three-dimensional world is extremely difficult. My goal for these vision descriptions is to provide greater awareness of places beyond for giving all of us wonderful opportunities to foster our spiritual growth. Our lives here are not an endpoint. We can be greatly comforted that the places we will experience on the other side are characterized by immense joy, peace, and loving warmth, and that choosing to grow spiritually has infinite, everlasting rewards.

Chapter I

Heaven's Light Energy

It has been an absolutely wonderful experience to have been blessed with the privilege to view nineteen places beyond our three-dimensional world. Life on the other side appears to be sustained by energies interacting from all dimensions, including ours, contacting each other, like a giant multiphase generator with power extremes well beyond our limited technological capabilities. The multiple levels of energies created from this massive assemblage of generative power direct the growth of the entire Universe, and are also available for us to tap into to direct our own soul growth.

I sensed from my visions that in the dimensions beyond, the life of the soul-body is sustained by energy that emanates from radiant, highly charged energy fields. The source of this energy is what John E. Moray calls the "Sea of Energy,"[2] and what physicists call zero-point energy. Hal Puthoff is the physicist who fathered and developed this concept, which he describes as being the abundant power residing in the vacuum of space, and which may explain "everything from gravity to atoms to the origin of the Cosmos itself."[3]

It is within this context that I believe we, as soul-body travelers, gather our energy from sources beyond our three-dimensional world. The soul-body energy molecules gather field strength from the essence of universal, quintessential cosmic energies. The product of our interactions with these cosmic energies is what produces our unique soul-body radiant signatures.

The process of dense and less dense matter, vibrating both in our present bodies and beyond in our soul-bodies, is *light*. Light is composed of a multiplicity of wavelengths, which our physical three-dimensional bodies have a limited capacity to sense. Our eye receptors can view only a fraction of the visible wavelengths in the total electromagnetic spectrum. A greatly extended reality exists in our natural environment and around other living organisms. This extended reality comprises a multitude of energy fields.

The vibrations of these energy fields are constantly interacting with our three-dimensional body sense receptors. These stimuli are transmitted to various parts of our brain, where electrical circuits are triggered to form patterns stored in brain matter. However, this process of storage extends beyond the physical.

In his book *Consciousness Beyond Life*, Pim van Lommel points out that there can be an "information transfer between matter and light through electron spin and nuclear spin resonance on the basis of nonlocal 'quantum entanglement.'"[4] Here, information is directly transferred between light and matter with consciousness being nonlocal in makeup.[5] He makes an excellent case for this in Chapter 13; his book is an extremely valuable and interesting read.

According to the thousands of documented "near death experiences" and "out of body experiences," there appears to be a recording and storage of our experiences in patterns of organized bioelectrical magnetic fields.

These fields, which encase our experiences, take on a life of their own to become self-sustaining. They gather energy from the universal energy flowing throughout the Universe. These fields of encasement comprise and preserve our soul-body or "Soul." This second body contains the sum total of all our experiences, gathered from every body vehicle we have used for temporary encasement, and this is the real you/us. This soul "energy body" has as its goal the quest for ultimate growth.

The special universal energy mentioned above, which flows throughout the Universe, appears to manifest itself in various forms of light. In his fascinating book *God at the Speed of Light: The Melding of Science and Spirituality*, T. Lee Baumann states that light is "one of the major forces present at the formation of the Universe," and that "countless references to light" appear within all the texts of the world's major religions.[6] From accounts describing creation to personal encounters with the paranormal and mystical perceptions, light is always present.

In my personal mystical impressions, everything involved spectacular light, which revealed my visionary images. Within each vision was a changing, glowing light that seemed to be very close to me, yet present everywhere. It was wonderfully intelligent and alive, expressing infinite comfort, compassion, and love. It reminded me of the beautiful resounding chorale for mixed voices composed by the mystical composer Jean Sibelius, *Onward, Ye Peoples!* The last phrase states, "and the heavenly choir doth ring from Mount Neboh, piercing the blue like a living light."[7]

The possibility of light being alive became very real to me with an unusual phenomenon known as the appearance of "orbs." A family acquaintance of ours has encountered them in her home and yard for years. One evening when she and a close realtor friend of ours were visiting with us, the conversation drifted onto the topic of "orbs." It was dark outside, except for a couple of high streetlights beaming from across the street, providing very dim background lighting. Standing in our front yard, our guest first concentrated for a few moments and then asked the "orbs" to appear. Incredibly, we all observed numerous glowing "orbs" within the branches of our large creosote bushes!

The unique glowing "orbs" did not appear to be a product of natural geophysical occurrences. We sensed them to be a living, intelligent phenomenon, a light alive—that is, each "orb" was a living light. These lights stemmed from energy within a hidden reality, perhaps an energy system different from the carbon-based cycle of life present in our three-dimensional world. We took many photos that night but have not been able to capture the orbs on camera since then.

The photographs below (photos, not illustrations) were taken in Scottsdale, Arizona in October of 2013 with a digital Kodak Easy Share DX 7630.

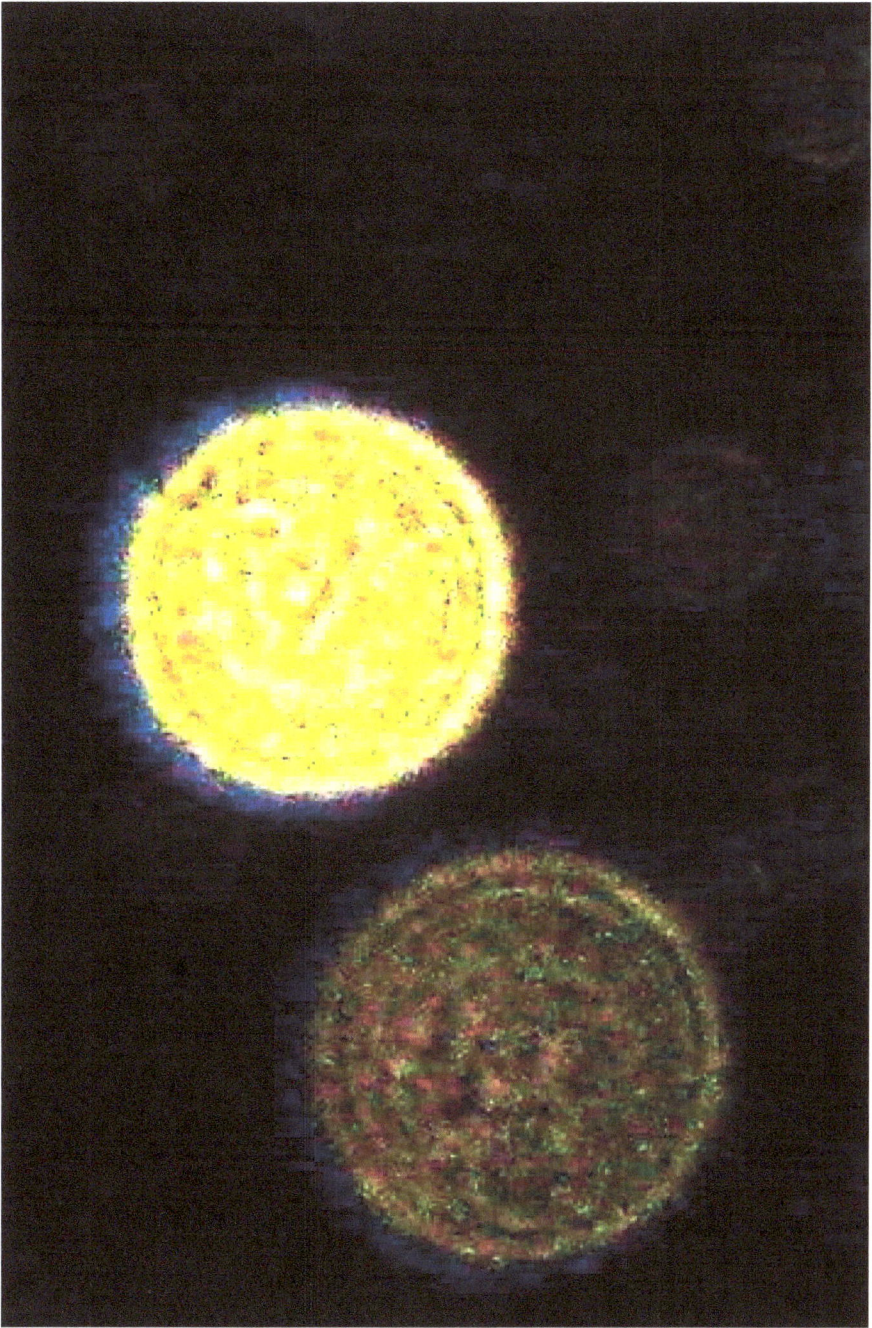

The following seven vision journeys were accompanied by a warm enveloping light. It felt alive and intelligent, and surrounded me with a deep sense of forgiving love, gentleness, kindness, and compassion. With each vision this all-knowing guiding light appeared to blend in harmony with each heavenly place I visited.

Chapter II

Vision Presentations

My seven-vision journey for enhancing soul vibrations begins with what I have named Choral Forest and ends with the Gallery of Multi-Dimensional Portals. All seven of these places transmitted unique vibrational resonance. The patterns of vibration assemblies were exclusive to each of the places they were generated from. These are centered on the general purpose of existence, which is to experience the great joy of alignment with the rays of light of the Creative Forces in the Universe.

I firmly believe that when a desire is present to expand the human elements of excellence described by enlightened people in all parts of our world, we become better aligned with those rays of light. Kahlil Gibran presents an elegant example. He challenges us to become *Chemists of the Heart*, where we direct our thoughts and behaviors to develop the best of human qualities to a greater depth. He suggests that we take the "heart's elements of compassion, respect, longing, patience, regret, surprise, and forgiveness and compound them into one … atom which is called LOVE."[8] Making this grand effort will truly help us evolve to what Pir Vilayat Inayat Khan, in his profound spiritual practice exercises, calls "Fashioning a Body of Light."[9]

The greatest challenge facing us is to figure out ways to implement and show the grand aspects of love in our daily lives here as well as in the afterlife.

Four great writers and their manuscripts have been a great help to me for deepening my understanding of these elements: Eric Fromm's book *The Art of Loving*,[10] Carl Rogers' book *On Becoming a Person*,[11] Annie Kirkwood's book *Mary's Message to the World*,[12] and the writings of the Dalai Lama in *The Dalai Lama: His Essential Wisdom*.[13] These authors, with their research and wisdom, are extremely enlightening for insightful and excellent living.

The seven places described next came to me from extended "One-point" meditation. I firmly believe that these places are waiting on the other side for us to explore, provided of course, that we choose to do so. The opportunities are always present for soul ascension here as well as there. I also have no doubt that there are countless other places I have not yet been able to visit through concentration on the white light guide within my mind.

May the following celestial journey be joyful and delightful as you wander through the seven "Mind-Mapped" visions. It may be interesting to try a re-visualization in your own mind as you read through the verbal descriptions.

Vision 1

Choral Forest

Choral Forest

The Choral Forest consisted of a colossal assembly of majestic trees. They formed an expansive grove of immense trunks with large attached branches forming archways of foliage. This gave the appearance of a monumental living cathedral extending in all directions, ascending hundreds of feet upward into a streaked skyline containing colors of lightly tinted gold and pale pink hues.

The tree varieties were not recognizable to me. Around the base of the trees and in the zones between them were extensive, beautifully proportioned flowers of all tints and shades of every possible color. Interspersed among and in between them were plants resembling ferns, long and symmetrical with multi-pointed tips and edges of varying textures. The whole array, in contrast to what we see in our three-dimensional world, was greatly augmented in a majestic manner characteristic of a magnificent painting. This rich blend of lush greenery, with its exquisite mix of color glittering all around, blended into a soft, light-brown lush carpet of unknown foliage. This was connected to all areas in patterns of intricate, multi-geometric forms.

The internal support structure of the trees was not completely solid, but rather their internal essence appeared to be composed of vibrating stationary energy fields. This phenomenon of stationary energy fields was prevalent and present in all of the visionary places I have experienced.

A particularly unique characteristic of this great forest was that the branches and foliage of the trees moved with an undulating, whispering resonance of blended sounds, similar to a series of soft harmonic chimes, creating a symphony of majestic music. The complex interaction of the sounds of these tree chimes created endless beautiful musical compositions. An unseen force seemed to be generated from inside each tree, with each tree being its own key on and within a giant keyboard, which was translated or transferred into a divine, magnificent concert experience. Encountering this was extremely calming, but electrifying and joyous at the same time. This grand phenomenon began immediately as one entered this stately, giant forest.

As I walked among these powerful trees, their thick branches, with profuse foliage attached, began to vibrate and sway like they were embracing each other. This transmitted to me a heightened feeling of great peace and tranquility, connecting my inner soul-self to a beautiful source, pouring out all-embracing love. Feeling love from these wonderful, powerful life-forms transmitted a rapture of ecstasy, which created a sense of wanting to be forever thankful to the great creative loving force that brought me and all life-forms into existence.

A walk through the Choral Forest provided an exceptional opportunity to renew and transform my consciousness toward a higher level of auric vibration. The great solace of the Choral Forest awakens the desire to experience an entirely new level of spiritual uplift. It is really a wonderful place to begin one's soul transformation journey for "Becoming" in the Light of Heaven.

Vision 2

Sea of Fields

Sea of Fields

When I emerged from my encounter with the Choral Forest, I crossed through a misty, translucent, wavy energy field. This led to a very smooth shoreline of very fine sand-grain material, light gold in color. Its texture was soft, but there was a gentle firmness to it. This material blended into what appeared to be low, rippling, shining waves. They had an interactive radiance from multiple forces of harmonic expressions, appearing to be some form of electrical field energy.

The intermingling of these electric-type fields formed something similar to a light gold mirage of changing energy waves. The difference being, in this case, that the energy waves did not disappear as you walked through them in a drifting manner. I felt them moving and enveloping me with a feeling of gentle warmth, a warmth that emanated mild exhilaration. It was a special atmospheric effect without the presence of heat; the warmth being generated was not from any heat source that we experience in our three-dimensional world. It warmed the soul-body within its structure, as well as touching its outer surface.

These gentle waves constantly changed in pastel brightness and light intensity relating to the color hues of blue and yellow-gold. Above this Sea of Fields was a slightly moving sky, which was an endless blend of pinks and whites. It was like a silky, expansive fabric moving along with the characteristic of a slow breeze, streaming off into an unknown horizon.

As I stepped into the gentle lapping waves, I did not sink down, but glided along their surfaces, feeling currents of energy within the waves. In addition to this effect, each movement produced the feeling of joyful elation, which moved like a gentle current flowing throughout one's whole soul-being. If you desired to stop moving and lie flat on the low rolling wave surface, it would feel like you were being carried along in a floating, soothing manner inside a fluffy cloud, with only a very light, hardly noticeable downward pulling force. This encounter harmonized and energized my whole soul-body's energy field.

Moving across the Sea of Fields, its point of termination became noticeable, where a bright pinkish white misty wall of cascading waves began to melt away into a narrow chasm. Through the center of the chasm I could see what looked like a shining bridge-way forming, tapering off to a point of light far beyond in the distance.

What was particularly characteristic of this vision was the close, overt presence of soft, moving energy fields. My other vision places were more distant, so I was not able to experience their energy emanations directly. However, I felt that the moving energy fields were denser than I could sense and had a definite form.

For my own clarification and in order to better comprehend what I saw and experienced in my Sea of Fields vision, I made a quick review of electrical field discoveries. I felt this to be of vital importance because I believe our trans-soul bodies may be composed of regenerative, resonant, stabilized electrical fields. These fields are present everywhere in our three-dimensional world, holding together the form and structure of matter, both organic and inorganic in composition. I further sense that the form and the structure present in other dimensions are also composed of sets of organized fields following definite patterns of order, controlled by electricity.

It is fascinating to note that according to Edgar Cayce, who many believe to be the most gifted psychic of all time, "all vibration becomes electrical in its action and effect" (Reading 2492-5). And also, "electricity or vibration is that same energy, same power, ye call God" (Reading 2828-4).[14]

Meanwhile two brilliant early scientists, Michael Faraday and Hans Christian Orsted, made key contributions in the development of the field of electrical science. Faraday discovered that the use of magnets produces a flow of electrons, which produces electricity. He also observed that any movement by a coil of wire interacting with a magnet breaks the magnetic lines of force, inducing a current of electricity. This led to the founding of our electrical industry.[15] And Orsted discovered that when an electrical current flows through a wire, it generates a circular magnetic field along with heat and light.[16]

Considering how electric fields are generated in our three-dimensional world, I believe something similar happens in other dimensions, which I have designated as the realms of Heaven. Heaven, I believe, can be defined as a series of electrical fields structured in zones which are generated and derived from particle fields of matter in a state of high vibration. The interaction of these fine energy field particles creates an ordered arrangement of fields to produce an environment for our soul-fields to interact with. This environment is composed of harmonic energy layers forming realities new and different from what we can sense directly with our three-dimensional sense receptors. These new realities could be likened to key signature changes with modulating, interconnecting "soul-field tuning places," where personal soul growth and ascension can occur if the entity so desires it.

I sensed that the Sea of Fields really carried the potential for soul refinement. The possibilities for spiritual energy accumulation and attunement for ascension are present here on Earth, but are magnificently present for us in heavenly places beyond. These few visions attempt to describe a small, partial picture of those splendid opportunities awaiting us. A further expansion of this conceptualization is discussed in Chapter IV.

Vision 3

Energy Falls

Energy Falls

Like each of the unique phenomena described in these visions, Energy Falls always projected into my consciousness a great flow of loving energy from an endless source. The Presence of this Source was continuously available to assist my consciousness to transcend further into a euphoric level of spiritual questing to encounter the new realities of these wonderful places in Heaven.

As the Sea of Fields narrowed into a chasm of cascading falls, I found myself walking on a pearlized silver-tinted walkway glistening with sparkling radiance, similar to a bridge without visible support. This extended forward toward a one-point shaft of light much brighter than the glow surrounding the borderless walkway.

The walkway curved slightly upward and could be designated as a bridge, since it seemed to transverse over a bottomless spray of mist. As I walked, my feet were gently stabilized as they made contact with the smooth, glossy surface, which had a very slight, springy softness. The bridge-way had an internally lit glow, the light of which faded into a dimly illuminated mist, becoming less illuminated to the indeterminable depth below.

The cascading waves of rushing, misty energy falling on both sides of the bridge-way filled my whole etheric body with exhilarating vibrations. The rushing, falling, misty waves were very close to the bridge-way. The massive falls on each side were multi-colored in appearance and continually streamed downward from a concealed source. These blended into a darkened skyline faintly illuminated by small, countless points of light sparkling like faceted diamonds, spread out on an expanse of soft black velvet. The bright light points appeared to be illuminated by the brightness of the bridge-way and the surrounding falls. Semi-cloudy, wispy mist from below appeared from time to time around the shining bridge-way, gently enveloping me.

Moving along the bridge expanse, I felt extremely exhilarated within my soul-form essence over and over again. Farther ahead, a very bright light was streaming from what appeared to be a portal. The light had a very warm, inviting sensation as I approached it. The portal seemed to be a great distance away, however not only was I moving, but the bridge-way was also moving toward it, making my inner sense of time for travelling there short.

When I passed through this shimmering concentric portal, I emerged into a magnificent group of towering structures, which formed a beautiful array of archways.

Vision 4

Archways of Energy Mist

Archways of Energy Mist

At a distance, the complex of arches looked like a painting containing colors ever-changing in new blends of vibrant, variegated brilliance.

Upon entering the Misty Archways, I felt the fine particle mist showering down in vibrating waves from the upper sections of the archways. This was similar to water vapor misters in our three-dimensional world, but instead of having an outside surface body sensation, I felt the fine misty particles of energy permeating my entire soul-being. This experience was the highest form of God's blessing, generating an exaltation of divine inner peace.

The beautiful misty archways were aesthetically arranged and designed to form interlocking porticos. These porticos had small extended walkways leading to the central promenade. The misty showers drifting down from the arches varied in color from light yellowish white to an intermix of turquoise-blue with tints of light purple.

The symmetrically elegant archways, which extended slightly downward from the portal's exit, spread out onto a grand promenade sparkling like highly polished white marble. Connected to the end of the grand promenade were the final three visionary places described next. Beyond these three exquisite structures, one could see an awe-inspiring complex of spires rising high into a light pink and azure blue skyline. These were intricate in architectural design, representing the highest form of aesthetics, forming a massive celestial cityscape.

The spires, often having many sides, appeared to glow from within, but also projected reflected light on their outside surfaces, which had a finish of finely cut gemstones. The light they radiated was composed of a myriad of tints and shades of light color hues, brightly illuminating the cityscape within its confines and the shimmering, translucent walls around it. I called this heavenly city "The City of Spires" in my first book, *Walking on the Shores of Heaven*; a short general description is presented there.

The City of Spires

Vision 5

Fountain of Divine Spirit

Fountain of Divine Spirit

Moving from the Archways of Energy Mist onto the broad, smooth, gleaming promenade, I observed three amazing places toward the end of the promenade. The promenade split into three sections leading into each one. Behind them and farther on was the magnificent City of Spires complex.

The first of these three structures I have designated the Fountain of Divine Spirit. It represents one of the holiest places that I have ever encountered in my vision questing. As I attempted to describe this place, I sincerely hope the reader can determine why I believe it to be a place where the "Breath of God" was present.

It contained an interlocking pattern of gloriously illuminated columns, each of which radiated spectacular ray-sprays of brilliant white light interspersed with blazing, intense, glowing beams. These moved up and down as if held by invisible patterns of stationary field energy. This powerful light energy appeared to be emanating from a consciousness of total love and compassion. Heavenly etheric soul-body vision would be required to fully sense this profound concentrated light display. The energy sprays were quite fluid with translucent vapors and were more concentrated around the column edges. From a distance the vaporous, brilliant light sprays intermixed, to form interlocking "S" shapes in between and around the columns, similar to energy shields.

Beautiful, triumphant sounds similar to many ringing chimes resounded within and all around the intertwining fountain structure. Along with these resounding chords of harmonic chimes were powerful beats of complex rhythms forming continuous, evolving musical compositions. These were similar to intricate fugues with inexpressible sublime, divine grandeur. It was as if God's force had its own heartbeat discharging unlimited, exultant, living energy over and over again. In other words, it could be the ultimate source for energizing and sustaining soul-life force forever.

At this point, I must turn to poetic description to transmit what is so difficult to describe in prose, in order to better present a semblance of what I experienced there. The following stanzas summarize this very powerful, personal, spiritual visionary experience.

Fountain of Divine Spirit

Vicissitude, solicitude, beatitude clear,
Resounding forth from a higher sphere.
Fugal anthems praising with powerful might,
Project out radiant sprays of celestial light.
Awesome volume of sublime compassionate force,
Radiates the highest love from the endless Source.

Moving within Living Energy's luminous glare,
Glorious splendor of spiritual life shines rare.
Projecting exalted images of spiritual thoughts,
Pouring into one's being the Divine affection so sought.
Creating conceptions for a more perfect spiritual self,
To sculpture our soul for the Supreme purpose to be felt.

With these beautiful images reflecting so clear,
Communicating life's end here – never to fear.
To see the Truth in our soul's past endeavors of plight,
Countless dawns and sunsets, setting and rising bright,
All souls are spread as aisles for creation's walks,
Joyfully accepting God's endless inspirational thoughts.

Vision 6

Empyreal Hall

Empyreal Hall

Across from The Fountain of Divine Spirit was a colossal structure, a meeting place, a gathering place for soul-beings to meet and greet. I have designated it "Empyreal Hall." A wide variety of soul-body forms were present in the hall, all vibrating and changing slightly in appearance, but maintaining forms similar to our many human bodies here on Earth.

Their body surfaces were semi-transparent and somewhat translucent in light color hues, radiating in varying intensity. Each was beautiful in a unique way, transmitting auric energy of warmth and personal peace. Many had faces of quiet contemplation, and others were smiling with acceptance and happiness which conveyed loving effervescence and vivacity.

What was so beautifully unique about this place and the other astonishing places I visualized in Heaven was that they embellished one's soul-field with an energy adornment most suitable for souls to interact with the energy signatures of those places. This occurred most wonderfully in the four entrances shaped like domed arches resting on their sides covered by three layered domes extending down to ground level.

As soul-beings passed through these entrances, they became endowed with a beautiful radiance that characterized them in a unique way, being adorned with garments of light-matter. Their soul-field bodies then began to glow softly and blended into a garment similar to a flowing robe or loose-fitting, one-piece gown. These occasionally changed in color hues, characteristic of the color nuances found in auras surrounding our physical bodies here in the third dimension.

It is interesting to note that all the places I have been so privileged to envision thus far in Heaven were characterized by a predominance of bright light color hues of pink, blue, and golden-yellow to very bright white. All structures had a semi-transparent, translucent glowing aspect, and this was also seen in the soul-bodies who interacted with these places.

The soul-bodies making contact with each other in Empyreal Hall displayed another interesting characteristic. When you or someone else spoke, the lips and mouth moved slightly, but the vocal sounds seemed to resonate from within them to within you rather than from an outside source toward you. Each voice had a soft, distinctive timbre of varied intonations which became translated within your perceptive awareness into a language you could instantly understand. It was a form of meta-thought transference, making perceptual communication occur instantaneously between sender and receiver, creating lucid images from thoughts.

The energy flowing in and around Empyreal Hall filled one's soul-being with peaceful, comforting vibrations. This phenomenon of changing harmonics for fine-tuning our souls is unique to each heavenly place awaiting our visit. The possibilities become endless for our spiritual refinement. The purpose for this refinement is to broaden and deepen our capacity to incorporate these special vibrations to transmit all levels of Love to others, and move toward greater harmony with the Divine.

On all four sides of this astounding Hall, wide, gradient steps narrowed to smaller entranceway steps, giving the viewer a one-point perspective effect. These led through the arched entranceways into a foyer, which extended into circular chambers forming the central interior. From these meeting chambers, spiraling, floating stairways led to multi-level platforms containing numerous meeting rooms. These were places for diverse discussions by anyone who wished to contribute their ideas, knowledge, and experiences from all dimensional levels. This Hall was a forum for souls to build tolerance, understanding, respect, and love for multiple soul-types in God's Universe.

Spiritual friendship was the innate desire for everyone gathered in Empyreal Hall. The encounters experienced there will be great opportunities for spiritual growth. Present in the Hall were many soul-beings of ascended spiritual growth, who radiated high patterns of vibration and had advance knowledge from other life spheres composed of different energy structures. This provided endless opportunities to explore the many aspects of God's vibrations. These vibrations appeared to form a super-structure of the highest of joyful energy resonating throughout the Universe. I have called this phenomenon "The Chimes of God."

In the process of experiencing this place and accepting the ultimate task of describing at least a partial semblance of what I visualized, I definitely received the sense from beyond that Empyreal Hall was one of many immense collective meeting places in Heaven.

These places had entranceways of shimmering yellow-white light leading to inner vistas of softer, glowing illumination. Upon entering, you could see an inward sky with the hue of light-blue turquoise suspended above radiant chambers. Empyreal Hall was like a crystal goblet pouring out living energy for spiritual insight. Its spiritual sanctums provided new communication formats for soulminds to expand and explore higher levels of consciousness. This provided every visitor there an opportunity to choose a spiritual framework to participate more effectively in the excellence of creation.

Vision 7

Gallery of Multi-Dimensional Portals

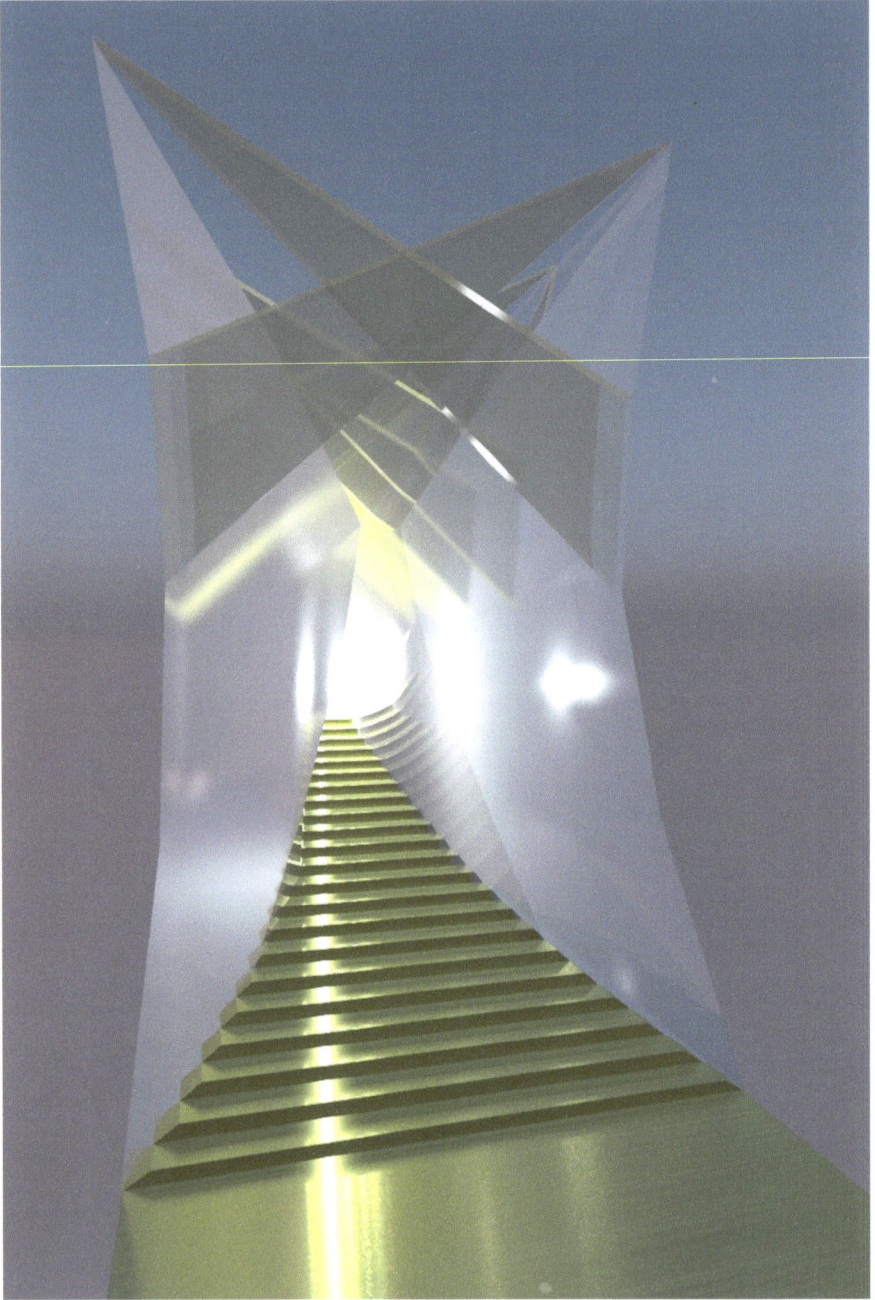

Left, Gallery entryway.
Next page, Gallery interior.

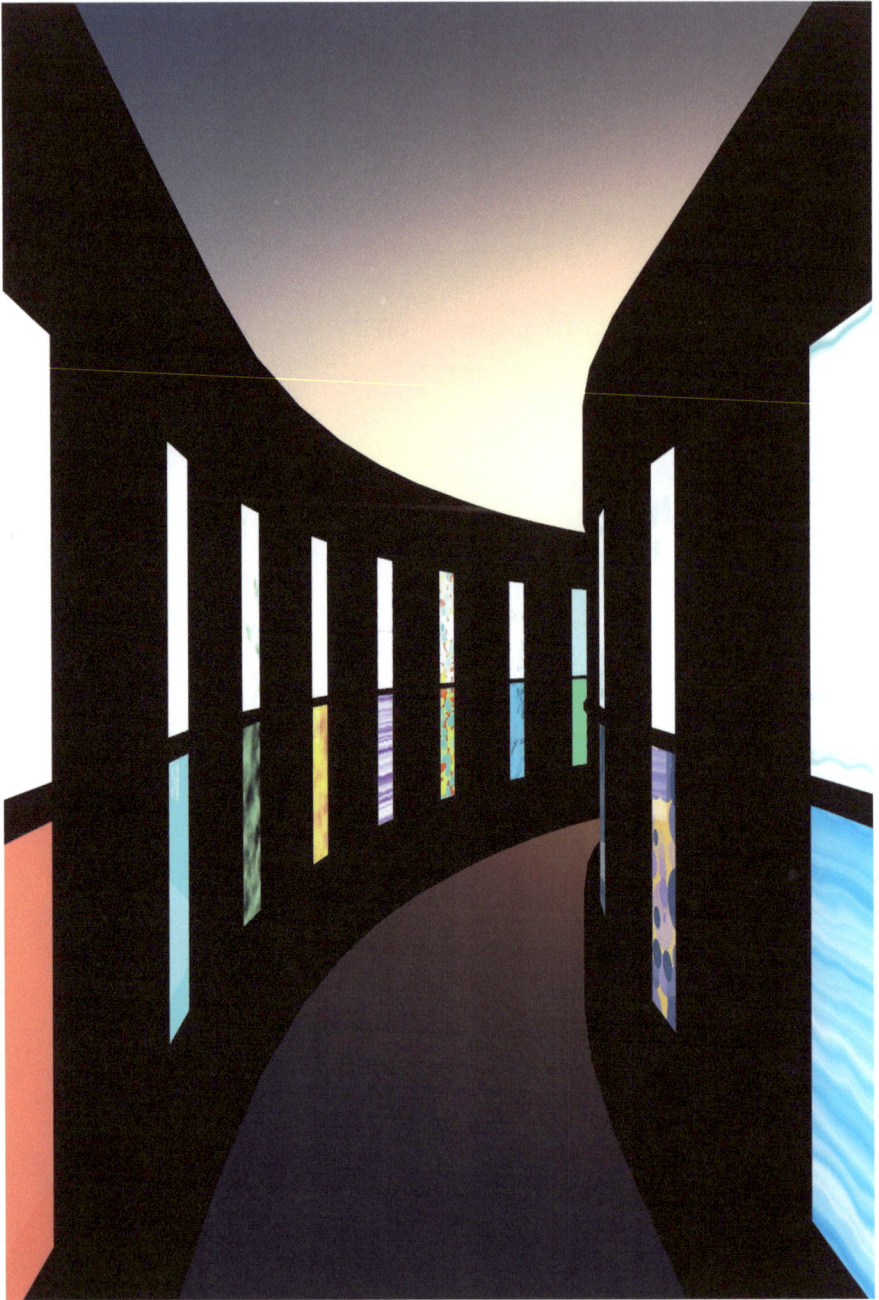

Gallery of Multi-Dimensional Portals

As I exited from the opposite side of Empyreal Hall, I saw off in the distance the "Gallery of Multi-Dimensional Portals." Leading into the Gallery was a long series of gentle golden steps, which were covered by modified V-shaped arches. These were sheltered under a large major dome of several gradient layers.

Inside the entrance vestibule was a mezzanine, which led to multiple linked passageways. These were organized in linear arrays extending in three directions, having no termination point in view. The arches forming the passageways emitted a soft, wavy light energy radiating iridescent glows from screens depicting a celestial place, city, or civilization.

Some of the screen content appeared similar to selective designs of ultra-modern architecture here on Earth; others were futuristic in a supernatural way. I was unable to get a very clear view of detail in any of them.

I discovered that it was not possible to step into or pass through any of these portals to certain heavenly places or realms unless one's soul energy field was in harmony with the energy framework surrounding the portal. A simple analogy here in our physically oriented three-dimensional world would be the following: If you wanted to cross a small lake, and the edges on each side were too steep to climb up and over, with a backward retreat also blocked, you would need the skills for swimming. Another example would be how magnets attract and repel each other depending upon the orientation of their field polarity.

In Heaven, we also need soul-body skills of various degrees of alignment and refinement to explore the countless different realms that exist there. Also, the degree to which we master our spiritual skills will determine the level of realms or places we can explore. To build ourselves through personal choices is a wonderful aspect of Heaven, as it is here on Earth, where beautiful places and experiences can be available to everyone desiring to energize the myriad behaviors displaying love. The sensation of "Great Love" is all-encompassing in all heavenly places. The opportunity to develop our "Soul Vibrational Keys" for spiritual development is always there. We always have that choice.

The Gallery of Multi-Dimensional Portals is a place of exceptional possibilities where souls can expand their spiritual potentials for creative ventures involving higher states of matter/energy exchanges. Although I was only able to view a few departure portals, I believe there were entry portals at the opposite end of the gallery. Perhaps all the places I have previously described may be places chosen to enter from other gallery locations.

As soon as one entered the foyer of the Gallery of Multi-Dimensional Portals, there were twelve glowing beings of light standing in what appeared to be a large panel of screens connected to Counselor Hall (which I visualized in my first book, *Walking on the Shores of Heaven*) and to a Divine Hall of Records, a place in Heaven that was contacted by Edgar Cayce. These beings had a very bright appearance. The upper half of their etheric body forms gleamed more brightly with wavy, varying tints of white and yellow-gold, giving the appearance of wings, but not actually having them affixed to their body essence. These beings were master empathic soul resonance readers. They could read, and directly experience, one's soul vibrations, the spiritual text level of accumulated thoughts.

This meant that they could guide, direct, and accompany one on their journey through a portal to another spiritual realm that would best enhance their soul growth. Like the beings of light in Counselor Hall, they could lovingly make suggestions, if it was the soul-being's choice, to help them choose the best destination for personal soul growth, and in some cases honor a soul's request to accompany them to that new destination. What a distinguished, noble calling they had, to be the Guides of God, consulting, translating, and directing us toward greater spiritual excellence in our soul's journey in the life to follow.

As we move forward in our spiritual evolution, we will experience great love, joy, and beauty far beyond what we can presently imagine and describe. This is what God, the Great Architect and Master of All Creative Forces has in store for us: to have this wonderful opportunity to move forward in His guiding light, to experience these great blessings found in creation over and over again.

Chapter III

Validity of Visions

One may ask the question, "Why should I believe that the seven visionary places in this book, along with the twelve described in my first book, *Walking on the Shores of Heaven*, are real?" If it were not for the very positive feedback I have been receiving for more than thirty years from people who have requested me to give "signature readings" for them, I might also have a certain degree of doubt. But according to feedback estimates, my accuracy has been running over 90 percent.

Signatures, I have discovered, mark significant aspects of soul-aura vibrations that are imprinted on the unified soul-field of each individual. My system for analysis is based on the musical form called the *fugue*, which involves a central notational theme with extended variations that complement the central theme form.

This great success in signature analysis has led me to accept the credence and validity of these visions; I feel humbled and very honored to have received them. I particularly appreciate the wonderful efforts of Charles Wolfsandle, my illustrator/artist, who was inspired in constructing a partial semblance of these spiritually enhancing places beyond.

Heaven appears to be a realm without limits, a place for continuous development. According to Annie Kirkwood in her beautifully written book *Mary's Message to the World*, Heaven is a place where we can continue to discover "the teaching's of God's Essence."[17] Annie's whole book emphasizes that the spiritual life is the total reality for us.[18] We can make choices to perfect our soul-being here on Earth, but Heaven offers limitless opportunities to delete the imperfections gathered from inaccurate past choices, and to acquire these qualities that represent the "Wholeness" of the Divine. The Divine is the guiding, creating, soul-field of energy that continually generates the composition and structure of all life-forms in the Universe—a vastness that lies well beyond what we humans can imagine.

Chapter IV

Forming a Theory of Heaven

During the course of my fifty years of personal investigations into scientific areas touching on metaphysics and cosmology, several areas of inquiry in particular have contributed key concepts for developing a theory of Heaven. I have tried in the following short discourse to integrate these key concepts in order to present a glimpse of what might describe and define the nature of Heaven.

In very broad terminology, I have defined Heaven as God's grandiose group of interlocking dimensions where soul life-forms in varying stages of being reside for continued personal development. From my personal visionary experiences thus far, Heaven appears to be a vast system comprising different levels of vibrational matter states, with the word *vibration* in this case meaning *varying periodic oscillation.*[19]

All of our elements, combining into compounds and mixtures with their sub-atomic components, have their own distinctive vibrations in our three-dimensional world. These atomic structures, I would like to propose, also form the base level for other dimensions. The fundamental vibrations from our three-dimensional matter interactions generate upper-level vibrational zones like "overtones or harmonics in music theory. Ratios of vibration are calculated from the pitch vibrations forming the 'Harmonic Series.'"[20] These varying harmonic expressions from our three-dimensional matter form other dimensions, which may be described as "spheres of overtones," producing what we designate as Heaven in the broad sense, as phrased in my opening general definition statement.

Within this broad definition, these overtone spheres or dimensions exist due to two factors: interstitial space between matter, and the endless "Sea of Energy," as John Moray calls it, which permeates the Universe.[21] The presence of these two factors provides the opportunity for organized energy fields to emerge, which can form realms of many different states of matter beyond our three-dimensional world.

These heavenly realms, according to my visions, appear to have definite patterns of organization characteristic of complex geometric designs. Realm designs indicate the influence of a mega-powerful Intelligence who appears to actually think non-living and living structures into existence. The force that the Super Intelligence may use for creation could be what several physicists have suggested: electrical currents with powerful magnetic whirlwinds.[22] According to Anthony Peratt—an electrical engineer and plasma physicist for the U.S. Dept. of Energy at the Los Alamos National Laboratory in New Mexico—the lab's supercomputer simulations have shown that these forces arise from gas-charged particles called plasma, and they are involved in shaping galaxies. This plasma, which appears to be everywhere in the cosmos, can create electrical filaments hundreds of millions of light-years long. When the filaments "tangle, twist, and break," galaxies and clusters of galaxies are formed.[23]

Proving this outside the use of supercomputers may not currently be possible, but nevertheless is quite intriguing for continued research. New astrological data are continuously coming in from ground and satellite-based telescopes. Regardless of the cosmological theory one accepts for the origin and structure of our Universe, radiation and radiant light have produced the necessary conditions for the creation of life in a myriad of forms represented on Earth. Cosmologists and astronomers have speculated that life may be abundantly present in many other star systems beyond our own.

In the outstanding book *God at the Speed of Light*, T. Lee Baumann, M.D. presents the case for light (in all its aspects), stating that there is a "direct link between light and the Supreme Designer of the Universe."[24] He further submits the proposition that only our senses limit us from experiencing dimensions beyond which we call spiritual, and which are predicted by quantum theory.[25] When our time comes to pass into these spiritual dimensions, I firmly believe in the premise that our energy field—which contains our consciousness (soul self)—continues its existence attached to an "energy field body." This energy field body is able to gather its life-sustaining energy from each respective dimension, each of which is connected to the universal energy flowing throughout the Universe.

It may be further conjectured, as suggested by Harvard University's celebrated theoretical physicist Sidney Coleman, that "just as quantum mechanics says there is a certain probability that particles can appear from nowhere in a vacuum, quantum cosmology says there may be a certain probability that a small chunk of space and time will suddenly pop into existence."[26] He further asserts that a wormhole is "a fluctuation in the space-time field, just as a virtual particle is a fluctuation in an energy field." Coleman believes there is no reason to make the assumption that our Universe is the only one. He posits that wormholes could connect to an infinite number of "preexisting parallel universes."[27] These wormholes could be the connecting sources for energy to flow into our Universe. One aspect of the energy flow from connecting wormholes might be information contributing to "values for the constants found in nature in our Universe."[28] Coleman's wormhole theory may be the key factor to explaining how "physics at the cosmic scale" can correspond to "physics at the quantum scale."[29]

According to Sam Flamsteed in his outstanding article "Crisis in the Cosmos," cosmological theories are thrown into a state of flux with each new astrological discovery.[30] The most exciting aspect of this, to me, is that fluctuation means movement. The occurrence of this at the quantum level, according to Dr. John Bahcall from the Institute for Advanced Study at Princeton, means that "we are all quantum fluctuations, and that's the origin of all of us and of everything in the Universe."[31] We are on an endless quest to understand the result of this quantum movement in creating reality as we perceive it.

The beautiful aspect of all the energy and particle processes occurring within our Universe is that these corresponding energy states are characterized by an orderly, stable interaction. Stephen Hawking succinctly summarizes this by stating, "If the world had been erected without the exclusion principle, quarks would not form separate, well-defined protons and neutrons."[32] The Austrian physicist Wolfgang Pauli was awarded the Nobel Prize in 1945 for his discovery of this principle, which basically states that "two similar particles cannot exist in the same state, that is, they cannot have both the same position and the same velocity, within the limits given by the uncertainty principle."[33] The Uncertainty Principle, widely accepted in physics, is broadly defined by Hawking as the concept that the position and velocity of a particle cannot be exactly known at the same time: "the more accurately one knows the one, the less accurately one can know the other."[34]

To clarify further, Hawking defines the exclusion principle as follows: "Two identical spin-½ particles cannot have (within the limits set by the uncertainty principle) both the same position and the same velocity."[35] Hawking then draws the conclusion that "without the Exclusion Principle … the structure of matter would all collapse to form a roughly uniform, dense soup."[36] Nevertheless, as T. Lee Baumann has pointed out in his wonderful book *God at the Speed of Light*, an Oxford mathematician by the name of Roger Penrose has calculated some startling statistics relative to the Universe's formation. He calculated that the odds of the Universe having been formed by chance are virtually negligible— his computations figured an odds ratio of 10^{300} to one against the possibility that the Universe was formed by chance.[37]

Theoretical mathematics can be a valuable tool to take us further in conceptualizing what lies beyond our third dimension. I believe this to be particularly relevant for forming a theory of Heaven. If living energy can populate our realm, then I believe it is entirely possible for living energy to exist in different dimensions beyond. We have body vehicles here, and we will have body vehicles there, adapted to experiencing life in those dimensions, matching our soul-body frequencies.

Theoretical mathematicians, along with physicists, have already brought us to a much closer understanding of the "fourth" dimension, which appears to be our closest neighbor touching those beyond.[38] In his article titled "Eleventh Dimension," Paul Davies summarized some brilliant ideas from the German physicist Theodor Kaluza, who proposed that what "we normally think of as an electromagnetic field is really part of a gravitational field in a four-dimensional space."[39] Kaluza's theory demonstrated that Einstein's gravitational field equations, when calculated in five-dimensional form, could be regrouped to construct a direct expression of four-dimensional gravitational equations. His work also shed light on the nature of electromagnetism as related to the weak and strong forces in physics. These three forces, along with gravity, appear to interact to form, according to theoretical physicists, a total of at least eleven space-time dimensions.[40]

Adding the dimension of time to the three dimensions we normally experience, leaves seven extra space dimensions beyond our ability to perceive. This field of inquiry is defined and described by excursions into Topology.[41] The existence of these seven other dimensions may be where we define Heaven, and the concept of them I find fascinating from the standpoint that a lot of space exists within and beyond our third dimension for Heaven to encompass.

The concept that dimensional space beyond our own third dimension can be proven to exist came into even better focus when a long-standing mathematical challenge in Topology was finally solved. After almost a century, the Poincaré conjecture was solved by Grigori Perelman, who introduced his proofs in three papers, in 2002 and 2003.[42]

The Poincaré conjecture states that "every simply connected, closed 3-manifold is homeomorphic to the 3-sphere."[43] Dr. Perelman developed theorems to solve the conjecture utilizing Richard Hamilton's suggestion to use what was designated the "Ricci Flow," *with surgery* on a closed oriented 3-manifold. This meant that spherical regions were systematically excised in a controlled way as they were developed. A number of mathematical teams have verified that Dr. Perelman's proof is correct.[44]

After a detailed review of his correct solution in 2006 by the Clay Mathematics Institute, Dr. Perelman was awarded the Millennium Prize of $1,000,000, and he received the Fields Medal on March 18, 2010. However, on July 1, 2010 he turned down the prize, saying very modestly that "he believes his contribution in proving the Poincaré conjecture was no greater than that of Hamilton's" (who first suggested using the Ricci Flow for the solution).[45]

Proving the Poincaré conjecture was the last link to validating the relationship between our three-dimensional world and "both dimension four and all higher dimensions."[46] For further reading and a detailed list of references discussing Dr. Perelman's papers, Wikipedia offers an excellent review.[47]

Whether an expansion into zones from our third dimension or composed of dimensions beyond our dwelling, Heaven appears to be where we reside before birth and after death. An energy exchange takes place in either case. We—as life energy fields with all variants of other life-forms—are attached to these energies through patterned gateways, capable of reproduction within and from a living interaction source.

In his book *The Soul of the Universe*, Mount Wilson astronomer Gustaf Stromberg posits the theory that life-forms comprise a guided pattern of energies. Stromberg brilliantly explores the process of life-forming patterns interacting with the composite matter of our biological being. The book cover quotes Albert Einstein giving his view of Stromberg's discourse: "Very few men could of their own knowledge present the material as clearly and concisely as he has succeeded in doing."[48]

Stromberg makes a strong case for our human brains being constructed as a synergetic system of "structures and vibrations" containing matter and hormones that supports living energy fields.[49] It "does not of itself produce mental qualities, but reproduces certain structural and non-structural cosmic qualities."[50] He proposes that "organizing fields" are guiding the growth and development of living biological organisms.[51] He expands further by expressing that "matter and life, and consciousness have their 'roots' in a world beyond space and time."[52] At discrete points in time, with the help of "guiding fields having space and time properties," both material particles and life-forms emerge to form what our senses perceive.[53]

A patterned pre-programming is definitely present here, in order for us to interact with shared perceptual congruence with our fellow human beings. Stromberg's second appendix, "Mind and Matter," summarizes the work of the brilliant German embryologist Hans Spemann, who describes the development of an embryo as being directly related to the action of an organizing field that emerges within the embryo itself, having the chief function of producing a nerve system. As the field expands, it is the agent responsible for the structure of the brain and our very complex interconnected nervous system. The interaction of this unfoldment is what determines the "functional and structural organization of our bodies."[54]

Dr. Stromberg continues to explain the wonderful nature of nerve cells as having two kinds of organizing energy fields: "the electrical fields inherent in all matter, and the living field characteristic for the organized living structures."[55] The fields of energy we call electrical are contained inside the elementary particles that form the atomic structures of atoms—the building blocks of the Universe.[56]

The sources of the living life-forming fields are different from the electrical fields in that they contain no "inherent rest-mass." These life fields expand during organismic growth from non-living chemical materials, and contract during the dying process. These life fields appear to be outside of space-time, their origin being in another world or dimension.[57] This compacted field energy, when it returns to or reenters another dimension, gathers energy from that dimension for development there.

The amazing thing is that our consciousness is attached to that energy field when it moves into the next dimension. This entry process has been documented by a large body of evidence presented by many researchers who have studied "Out of Body Experiences" (OBEs) and "Near Death Experiences" (NDEs). Thousands of these experiences have been documented from around the world, and many are available in books and from online sources.

Although a discussion of this literature would be well beyond the scope of this text, three noteworthy books nevertheless present some highly interesting and informative material relating to investigations of the NDE and OBE phenomena: *The Vestibule* by Jess E. Weiss, *Life After Life* by Raymond A. Moody Jr., and *Consciousness Beyond Life* by Pim van Lommel, M.D. The research and testimonials presented in these books may bring the reader to an awareness of the extraordinary possibilities waiting for us beyond.

Heaven appears to be our home before birth and after death, where an energy exchange takes place in both events. As life energy souls, along with all the variety of other life forms on earth, we are attached to these soul energies. Through patterned dimensional entrances we can pass from Heaven to earth and back to Heaven as our time here is fulfilled. Other scientists have also proposed the possibility of this soul energy flow.

This discussion has focused on the key concept that what we are, and how we came into existence, does not happen by chance. According to theoretical mathematics, the probability that our Universe has been unguided in its process of unfoldment is astronomically low. A grand design with the Grand Designer therefore appears to be present. It appears that the grand design of reality does not end just with our experiences in the three-dimensional world. It is one of many dimensions contained within the larger reality that makes up our Universe, and Heaven resides in those dimensions, of which ours is one zone. A synopsis of Heaven would include zones that appear to have their own distinctive harmonic vibrations, similar to key signatures in music, as mentioned in Chapter II.

To move from one key signature to another requires a harmonic adjustment in resolution similar to transitional chord modulations in music. In other words, there must be an adjustment in "field strength" or level of vibration of energy/matter. This is necessary to move the level of one's soul field to match the key vibrational signature of that other dimension's frequency vibration. I would call this a spiritual harmonic progression toward soul ascension. This advancement to another level of consciousness requires a definitive decision to "want to become," to be attuned and in harmony with a new, higher plane. Of course, remaining where we are is also a choice, unless our body vehicle wears out, as is the case in our three-dimensional world. However, there are many levels of consciousness we can choose from during our existence here.

One beautiful aspect of all this is that I sensed the presence of doorways being always open to us. It is our choice to achieve and become, and this will happen—as countless inspirational writers and speakers have declared—when we make choices to promote the various levels of "loving service" to each other.

Our human voice may indeed be the most useful instrument for promoting soul growth in ourselves and others through verbal communication. The reverse may also be true if ill will and anger are present when we speak. The presence of goodwill, kindness, and softness of tone in the communication process encourages positive personal growth. This, I believe, is the primary goal that we must continually explore in order to develop our spiritual potentials.

Chapter V

Developing Spiritual Growth by Transmitting Goodwill

My search for fundamental concepts about the development of spiritual potentials led me to an exciting and significant book by Fosar Grazyna and Franz Bludorf titled *Vernetzte Intelligenz*. In short, the key part of the text states the following:

> There is evidence for a whole new type of medicine in which DNA can be influenced and reprogrammed by words ... [and] that the alkalines of our DNA follow a regular grammar and do have set rules just like our languages.[58]

In other words, the science of the future may be something called "wave genetics," which carries the potential to be world transforming. The application of specific vibrations and language can result in "cutting out" or "reintroducing single genes from the DNA."[59]

In light of this cutting-edge research, it seems vitally important to think carefully about what we want to or should say, before we speak. The way we express our language in the human voice can significantly affect the quality of another person's being to either limit or actualize the personal and spiritual growth of that person.

The timbre and choice of our words combined with the positive intention of *goodwill* is the key growth-producing aspect of any verbal exchange. It is crucially important that before speaking, we must ask ourselves whether or not our ideas and images—which we translate into language—will reflect an expression of what is good and excellent for the receiver to hear. With the intention of goodwill behind our spoken words, the possibilities for spiritual growth become optimal for both the sender/ speaker and receiver/listener.

We must next consider what will help us to develop a positive verbal exchange that engenders mutual goodwill. Psychologists tell us that personal growth occurs when people interact without adopting false fronts or façades— when they are being genuine. The master therapist Carl Rogers calls this "congruence."[60] This factor, along with having a warm, accepting manner of behavior—an outgoing positive intention without reservations, with "empathic understanding"—creates a viable process for optimal personal growth to occur.[61]

These factors become actualized as spiritual potentials when a person makes a conscious decision always to try to engage them in the verbal communication process. Goodwill, in its broadest sense, is the catalyst for multiplying behavioral patterns of excellence, leading to our own self-growth as well as that of others. It also creates the right environment for the formation of spiritual ideals that can guide us here and in the hereafter to levels of joy and happiness beyond what we ever dreamed possible.

According to the modern composer and vocalist Meredith Monk, "you only leave love behind." And also, "curiosity is an antidote of fear."[62] Along with these two insightful comments she has also remarked that "all human beings are part of a vocal family, and the human voice is our human instrument."[63] She proposes that the making of music is a vital key for personal awakening and transcendence.[64]

Chapter VI

Meditation for World Light

We can use our consciousness to raise the vibration of our planet by concentrating on receiving energy from the "Great Love" that is present everywhere in the Universe. This Great Love is what grants us access to the energy that powers our souls. This energy sustains the angels and the beings that are present in every realm.

Having the highest desire for Goodwill is what enables us to attract the vibrations of higher light. Single-mindedly concentrating on Good Will empowers the capacitor within our soul-being to collect the higher light energies. We can then apply this energy to help uplift our chosen subject, as described in the following suggested meditation.

****

Take a few moments to still your mind and then imagine a place of great natural beauty, where you are resting comfortably, surrounded by a warm, radiant light. This may be a garden, a field of flowers, a soft grassy meadow leading off into a bright horizon, or some other place in your own imagination. Picture yourself sitting or lying flat on your back in this beautiful place, with a glowing light moving slowly like a wave of energy from the tip of your toes to the top of your head. Picture it crystallizing all the cells of your body into sparkling light with the appearance of diamonds shining outward with glistening brilliance.

After residing in this magnified, illuminated state of being for a few minutes, rub your hands together vigorously for about 20 seconds. Pull them apart slowly and imagine a shining ball of white light being generated between them. Imagine that you are actually holding the globe of our planet Earth suspended in this glowing ball of beautiful white light.

Think of our Earth in the most kind, gentle, loving way you can imagine, moving your hands to caress it softly, as if it were the most precious living entity you possess. Think repeatedly of giving it love, peace, and kindness, and of making it more beautiful. Work with this image for several minutes before letting it fade gradually around the object in your mind's eye.

Alternatively, when you have achieved the image of the glowing globe of white light between your hands, split it into two globes, holding one in each hand. With these two globes, imagine your body is to be expanded to the size of a powerful, angelic being reaching around the whole Earth, connecting the two globes of shining white light. This will create a band of radiant etheric energy that is generating Goodwill, love, and spiritual peace.

This meditation practice can also be applied to a particular person or small group of people, using a photograph or a clear mental image and picturing them within your energy globe. When the energy field ball feels sufficiently strong and bright between the span of your hands, you can impart all those beneficial qualities to whomever you choose. You must be very attentive to retaining only beneficial thoughts and images.

Your free will combined with positive intention can be a powerful tool for enhancing the well-being of people and even animals and plants. What more wonderful gift can we impart to the living world than to picture it as a dynamic, living domain that is receiving kindness, beauty, wonderful health, and loving affection!

"We [who] descended from great causal spheres of rainbowed light-souls are we who once surveyed worlds within worlds in the Being of God."

– Elizabeth Clare Prophet,
The Lost Teachings of Jesus [65]

Notes

[1] Deepak Chopra. 1995. *The Return of Merlin*, p. 393. Harmony, Crown, New York.

[2] John E. Moray. 2012. *The Sea of Energy in Which the Earth Floats*. Xlibris Corp., T. Henry Moray Foundation, P.O. Box 58141, Salt Lake City, UT, 84158-0141.

[3] Owen Davies. 1991. "Volatile Vacuums," *Omni*, vol. 13, no. 5 (February): 50–52.

[4] Pim van Lommel, M.D. 2010. *Consciousness Beyond Life: The Science of the Near Death Experience*, pp. 276–277. Harper Collins, New York.

[5] Ibid., p. 276.

[6] T. Lee Baumann. 2001. *God at the Speed of Light: The Melding of Science and Spirituality*, p. 39. ARE Press, Virginia Beach, VA.

[7] Jean Sibelius. 1939. *Onward Ye Peoples!* Arranged by Channing Lefebvre. Galaxy Music Corp., New York.

[8] Anthony R. Ferris, editor and translator. 1962. *Spiritual Sayings of Kahlil Gibran*, p. 27. Citadel Press, New York.

[9] Pir Vilayat Inayat Khan. 1999. *Awakening, A Sufi Experience*, p. 96. Jeremy P. Tarcher/Putnam, Penguin, New York.

[10] Eric Fromm. 1956. *The Art of Loving*. Harper & Row, New York.

[11] Carl R. Rogers. 1961. *On Becoming a Person*. Houghton Mifflin, Boston.

[12] Annie Kirkwood. 1991. *Mary's Message to the World*. G. P. Putnam's Sons, New York.

[13] Carol Kelly Gangi, editor. 2007. *The Dalai Lama: His Essential Wisdom*. Fall River Press, New York.

[14] Barbara A. Robinson. 1958. "Secrets of the Lost Ark," *Venture Inward*, vol. 27, no. 2 (2011): 23.

[15] William C. Vergara. 1958. *Science in Everyday Things*, p. 235–237. Harper & Brothers, New York.

[16] Hans Christian Orsted. Wikipedia. Retrieved March 2011. http://en.wikipedia.org/wiki/Hans_Christian_Orsted

[17] Annie Kirkwood. 1991. *Mary's Message to the World*, p. 196. G.P. Putnam's Sons, New York.

[18] Ibid., p. 114.

[19] Ebeneze Prout. 1903. *Harmony: Its Theory and Practice*, pp. 322–327. Augener, London.

[20] Ibid., pp. 124–125.

[21] Moray, *The Sea of Energy in Which the Earth Floats*.

[22] Sharon Begley. 1988. With Michael Rogers and Karen Springer, "Where the Wild Things Are," *Newsweek* (June 13): 60–65.

[23] Ibid., p. 65.

[24] Baumann, *God at the Speed of Light*, p. 38.

[25] Ibid., p. 138.

[26] Sidney Coleman, quoted by David H. Freedman in "Maker of Worlds," *Discover*, vol. 11, no. 7 (July 1990): 46–52.

[27] Ibid., p. 50.

[28] Ibid.

[29] Ibid., p. 52.

[30] Sam Flamsteed. 1995. "Crisis in the Cosmos." *Discover*, vol. 16, no. 3 (March): 66–74.

[31] Dr. John Bahcall, cited in John Van Auken, "We Are Stardust: Scientists See Our Stellar Origins," *Venture Inward Newsletter* (Winter 2011): 1–2. Association for Research and Enlightenment, Virginia Beach, VA.

[32] Stephen Hawking. 1988. *A Brief History of Time: From the Big Bang Theory to Black Holes*, pp. 67–68. Bantam Books, New York.

[33] Ibid.

[34] Ibid., p. 187; see also pp. 54–55 regarding the "Uncertainty Principle."

[35] Ibid., pp. 68, 184.

[36] Ibid., p. 68.

[37] Baumann, *God At the Speed of Light*, p. 124.

[38] Gerry Segal. 1984. "The Fourth Dimension." *Science Digest*, vol. 92, no. 1 (January): 69.

[39] Paul Davies. 1984. "The Eleventh Dimension." Science Digest, vol. 92, no. 1 (January): 72.

[40] Ibid.

[41] Ibid.

[42] Poincaré Conjecture, *Wikipedia, The Free Encyclopedia*. https://en.wikipedia.org/wiki/Poincaré_conjecture, p. 1.

[43] Ibid.

[44] Ibid.

[45] Ibid.

[46] Ibid., p. 4.

[47] Ibid., pp. 7–11.

[48] Gustaf Stromberg. 1970. *The Soul of the Universe*. Educational Research Institute, North Hollywood, CA.

[49] Ibid., p. 249.

[50] Ibid.

[51] Ibid., pp. 250–253.

[52] Ibid., p. 253.

[53] Ibid.

[54] Ibid., p. 258.

[55] Ibid.

[56] Ibid.

[57] Ibid., pp. 258–259.

[58] "Words," in this case, relates to specific vibrational patterns that promote healing and health. Fosar Grazyna and Franz Bludorf, *Vernetzte Intelligenz*, pp. 1–8. Summary and commentary by Baerbel (available only in German). ISBN 3930243237. Author contact www.fosar-bludorf.com: Transmitted by Vitae Bergman. Retrieved November 17, 2008. www.ryze.com/view.php?who=vitaeb. Reference http://www.bethcoleman.net/intelligence.html. (ISBN 3930243237)

[59] Ibid.

[60] Carl Rogers. 1963. "Learning To Be Free," in *Conflict and Creativity* by Seymour M. Farber and Roger H. L. Wilson, pp. 274–275. McGraw-Hill, New York.

[61] Ibid.

[62] Meredith Monk interview. 2012. *On Being*. KUHF Public Radio, Houston, TX. Host Krista Tippett, Feb. 19.

[63] Ibid.

[64] Ibid.

[65] Elizabeth Clare Prophet. 1986. *The Lost Teachings of Jesus, 1*, p. 102. Summit University Press.

www.ingramcontent.com/pod-product-compliance
Lightning Source LLC
Chambersburg PA
CBHW042124080426
42733CB00002B/4